The Ultimate Guide to Crafting Crochet Magic

A Must Have Book for Newcomers

Ruby T Pedro

THIS BOOK BELONGS TO
The Library of

....

....

I can't tell you how grateful I am that you decided to read my book. My most heartfelt thanks that you took time out of your life to choose my work and I hope you find benefit within these pages.

There are so many books available today that offer similar content so that makes it even more humbling that you decided to buying mine.

Tell me what you thought! I am eager to hear your opinion and ideas on what you read as are others who are looking for a good book to buy. Leave a review on Amazon.com so others can benefit from your wisdom!

With much thanks.

Table of Contents

SUMMARY

The Timeless Art of Crochet: A Glimpse into its History:

Crochet, a craft that involves creating fabric by interlocking loops of yarn or thread with a hooked needle, has a rich and captivating history that spans centuries. From its humble beginnings to its current status as a beloved pastime, crochet has evolved and adapted, leaving a lasting impact on the world of textiles.

The origins of crochet can be traced back to the early 19th century, although some argue that its roots can be found even earlier in ancient cultures. The exact origins of crochet are somewhat shrouded in mystery, as it is difficult to pinpoint a specific time or place where it first emerged. However, it is widely believed that crochet developed as a way to imitate the delicate lacework that was popular during the Renaissance period.

In the 19th century, crochet gained popularity as a practical and decorative craft. It was often used to create intricate lace collars, cuffs, and edgings for clothing. Crochet patterns were passed down through generations, with each family adding their own unique touch to the craft. As the Industrial Revolution took hold, crochet became more accessible to the masses, as patterns and materials became more readily available.

During the Victorian era, crochet experienced a surge in popularity, becoming a fashionable pastime for women of all social classes. Crochet patterns were published in women's magazines, and women would gather in social circles to share their latest creations and exchange patterns. Crochet became a symbol of femininity and domesticity, with women often creating elaborate doilies, tablecloths, and bedspreads to adorn their homes.

In the early 20th century, crochet took on a new role as a form of self-expression and rebellion. The Arts and Crafts movement embraced crochet as a way to create unique and handmade items in a world increasingly dominated by mass production. Crochet was used to create bold and innovative designs, breaking away from the traditional lacework of previous eras.

Throughout the 20th century, crochet continued to evolve and adapt to changing trends and styles. From the bohemian crochet garments of the 1960s and 1970s to the modern and minimalist designs of today, crochet has remained a versatile and timeless art form. With the rise of the internet, crochet enthusiasts from around the world can now connect and share their passion for the craft, leading to a resurgence in popularity.

The Joy of Crafting and the Benefits of Crocheting: Crafting is a popular pastime that brings joy and fulfillment to many individuals. One particular craft that has gained significant attention and appreciation is crocheting. Crocheting involves using a hook and yarn to create various items such as blankets, scarves, hats, and even intricate designs. The process of crocheting not only allows individuals to express their creativity but also offers numerous benefits for their mental, emotional, and physical well-being.

First and foremost, crocheting is a highly enjoyable activity that brings a sense of joy and satisfaction. The process of transforming a simple ball of yarn into a beautiful and functional item is incredibly rewarding. The repetitive motions of crocheting can be soothing and meditative, providing a sense of calm and relaxation. This can be particularly beneficial for individuals who experience stress, anxiety, or other mental health issues. Engaging in crocheting can serve as a form of therapy, allowing individuals to focus their attention on the task at hand and temporarily escape from the pressures of daily life.

Furthermore, crocheting offers a creative outlet for self-expression. With countless patterns and designs available, individuals can choose to follow a pattern or create their own unique creations. This allows for personalization and the opportunity to showcase one's individual style and creativity. Crocheting can be a means of self-discovery and exploration, as individuals experiment with different colors, textures, and techniques to bring their visions to life. The sense of accomplishment that comes from completing a crocheted project is immeasurable and can boost one's self-esteem and confidence.

In addition to the mental and emotional benefits, crocheting also has physical advantages. The repetitive hand movements involved in crocheting can improve fine motor skills and hand-eye coordination. This can be particularly beneficial for individuals with arthritis or other conditions that affect dexterity. Crocheting can also serve as a form of exercise for the hands and fingers, promoting flexibility and strength. The act of crocheting can be a gentle and enjoyable way to keep the hands active and engaged, especially for individuals who may have limited mobility or are recovering from injuries.

Moreover, crocheting fosters a sense of community and connection. Many individuals who crochet join online communities, attend local crafting groups, or participate in charity projects. These communities provide a platform for individuals to share their passion for crocheting, exchange ideas, and offer support and encouragement.

How This Guide Aims to Transform a Novice into a Skilled Crocheter: This comprehensive guide is designed to take a complete novice and guide them through the process of becoming a skilled crocheter. Whether you have never picked up a crochet hook before or have dabbled in the craft but want to improve your skills, this guide is here to help you every step of the way.

The first section of this guide focuses on the basics of crochet. It starts with an introduction to the different types of crochet hooks and yarns available, helping you understand which ones are best suited for your projects. From there, it delves into the fundamental stitches, such as the chain stitch, single crochet, double crochet, and more. Each stitch is explained in detail, with clear instructions and accompanying visuals to ensure you grasp the technique correctly.

Once you have mastered the basic stitches, the guide progresses to more advanced techniques. It covers topics such as increasing and decreasing stitches, creating different textures and patterns, and working in the round. These skills are essential for tackling more complex projects and will greatly expand your crochet repertoire.

In addition to teaching the technical aspects of crochet, this guide also provides valuable tips and tricks to enhance your crocheting experience. It offers advice on choosing the right yarn for your projects, understanding crochet patterns, and troubleshooting common mistakes. It also includes guidance on proper tension and hand positioning, which are crucial for achieving neat and consistent stitches.

To further support your learning journey, this guide includes a variety of beginner-friendly crochet patterns. These patterns are specifically chosen to help you practice and apply the skills you have learned. Each pattern is accompanied by step-by-step instructions, detailed stitch counts, and helpful tips to ensure your success.

Furthermore, this guide emphasizes the importance of practice and patience. Crocheting is a skill that takes time to develop, and this guide encourages you to embrace the learning process. It provides suggestions for practice exercises and encourages you to experiment with different yarns, stitches, and patterns to further refine your skills.

By the end of this guide, you will have transformed from a novice crocheter to a skilled and confident one. You will have a solid foundation in crochet techniques, the ability to read and understand patterns, and the confidence to tackle more complex projects. Whether you want to create beautiful garments, cozy blankets, or intricate amigurumi, this guide will equip you with the skills and knowledge to bring your crochet visions to life.

Essential Crochet Tools and Materials Every Beginner Needs: When it comes to starting a new hobby like crochet, it's important to have the right tools and materials to ensure a successful and enjoyable experience. Whether you're a complete beginner or have some basic knowledge of crochet, having the essential tools and materials will make your journey into this craft much smoother.

First and foremost, you'll need a set of crochet hooks. These come in various sizes, ranging from small to large, and are typically made of metal, plastic, or wood. It's a good idea to invest in a set that includes a range of sizes, as different projects may require different hook sizes. Additionally, ergonomic crochet hooks are available for those who may experience discomfort or pain in their hands while crocheting.

Next, you'll need yarn. Yarn comes in a wide variety of colors, textures, and weights, so it's important to choose the right type for your project. For beginners, it's recommended to start with a medium-weight yarn, as it's easier to work with and provides good stitch definition. Acrylic yarn is a popular choice for beginners due to its affordability and wide availability. However, as you progress in your crochet journey, you may want to experiment with different types of yarn, such as cotton or wool, to achieve different effects in your projects.

In addition to crochet hooks and yarn, you'll also need a few other tools to complete your crochet kit. One essential tool is a pair of scissors for cutting yarn. It's important to have a dedicated pair of scissors for your crochet projects to avoid dulling your regular household scissors. Another useful tool is a yarn needle, also known as a tapestry needle, which is used for weaving in loose ends and sewing pieces together. A stitch marker is also handy for keeping track of your stitches, especially when working on larger projects.

To keep your crochet projects organized and easily accessible, it's a good idea to invest in a crochet bag or storage case. These come in various sizes and designs, and often have compartments and pockets to hold your hooks, yarn, and other tools. Having a dedicated storage solution will not only keep your supplies in one place but also protect them from dust and damage.

Lastly, it's important to have access to crochet patterns and instructional resources. There are countless books, websites, and online tutorials available that provide step-by-step instructions and inspiration for crochet projects. These resources can help you learn new stitches, techniques, and patterns, and guide you through the process of creating beautiful crochet

Introduction to Yarn: Types, Weights, and Color Selection of Crochet:

Crochet is a popular craft that involves creating fabric by interlocking loops of yarn using a crochet hook. One of the most important aspects of crochet is selecting the right yarn for your project. Yarn comes in various types, weights, and colors, each with its own unique characteristics and uses.

When it comes to types of yarn, there are several options to choose from. Acrylic yarn is a synthetic yarn that is widely available and affordable. It is known for its durability and easy care, making it a popular choice for beginners. Wool yarn, on the other hand, is made from the fleece of sheep and is known for its warmth and softness. It is a great choice for cozy winter garments and accessories. Cotton yarn is another popular option, known for its breathability and ability to absorb moisture. It is often used for making lightweight garments and home decor items. Other types of yarn include bamboo, silk, and alpaca, each with its own unique properties and uses.

Yarn weight is another important factor to consider when selecting yarn for your crochet project. Yarn weight refers to the thickness of the yarn and is categorized using a numbering system. The most common yarn weights are lace, fingering, sport, worsted, and bulky. Lace weight yarn is very thin and delicate, while bulky weight yarn is thick and chunky. The weight of the yarn you choose will depend on the type of project you are working on and the desired outcome. For example, if you are making a delicate lace shawl, you would choose a lace weight yarn, while a cozy winter blanket would require a bulky weight yarn.

Color selection is also an important aspect of crochet. The color of the yarn can greatly impact the overall look and feel of your project. When choosing colors, it is important to consider the intended use of the item you are making. For example, if you are making a baby blanket, you may want to choose soft pastel colors. If you are making a statement piece, you may opt for bold and vibrant colors. Additionally, it is important to consider color combinations and how they will work together in your project. Some crocheters prefer to use a single color for their projects, while others enjoy working with multiple colors to create intricate patterns and designs.

Understanding Crochet Hooks and Their Sizes:

Crochet is a popular craft that involves creating fabric by interlocking loops of yarn using a crochet hook. The crochet hook is an essential tool in this craft, as it determines the size and tension of the stitches. Understanding the different sizes of crochet hooks is crucial for achieving the desired outcome in your crochet projects.

Crochet hooks come in various sizes, ranging from small to large. The size of a crochet hook is denoted by a letter or a number, which indicates the diameter of the hook's shaft. The most commonly used sizing systems are the lettered system (US) and the metric system (mm). In the US system, the sizes range from B (2.25mm) to S (19mm), while in the metric system, the sizes range from 2.0mm to 25mm.

The size of the crochet hook you choose depends on the type of yarn and the desired outcome of your project. Thinner yarns require smaller hooks, while thicker yarns require larger hooks. Using the wrong size hook can result in stitches that are too tight or too loose, affecting the overall appearance and drape of the fabric.

To determine the appropriate crochet hook size for your project, you can refer to the yarn label or a crochet hook size chart. Yarn labels often provide a recommended hook size for that particular yarn. However, keep in mind that personal tension and gauge can vary, so it's always a good idea to make a gauge swatch before starting a project.

Crochet hook size charts are handy references that provide a range of recommended hook sizes for different yarn weights. They help you choose the right hook size based on the yarn weight and the type of project you're working on. These charts typically include information on the recommended hook size for each yarn weight category, such as lace, fingering, sport, worsted, and bulky.

In addition to the size, crochet hooks also come in different materials, such as aluminum, steel, plastic, and wood. Each material has its own unique characteristics and advantages. Aluminum hooks are lightweight and glide smoothly through the yarn, making them popular among beginners. Steel hooks are often used for fine thread crochet projects. Plastic hooks are lightweight and comfortable to hold, while wooden hooks provide a warm and natural feel.

It's important to note that crochet hook sizes can vary slightly between different manufacturers.

Grasping Basic Crochet Terms and Abbreviations: Learning the fundamental crochet terms and abbreviations is essential for anyone who wants to delve into the world of crochet. These terms and abbreviations serve as a universal language among crocheters, allowing them to understand and follow patterns, communicate with other crocheters, and expand their crochet skills.

One of the first things beginners need to grasp is the difference between a stitch and a stitch abbreviation. A stitch refers to the actual physical action of creating a loop with the yarn and pulling it through other loops to form a pattern. On the other hand, a stitch abbreviation is a shortened form of the stitch name used in crochet patterns. For example, the single crochet stitch is often abbreviated as "sc," while the double crochet stitch is abbreviated as "dc." Understanding these abbreviations is crucial when reading and interpreting crochet patterns.

Another important aspect of crochet terms and abbreviations is understanding the different types of stitches. There are numerous stitches in crochet, each with its own unique abbreviation. Some common stitches include single crochet (sc), double crochet (dc), half double crochet (hdc), and treble crochet (tr). Each stitch creates a distinct texture and appearance in the finished project, allowing crocheters to create intricate and beautiful designs.

In addition to stitch abbreviations, crochet patterns often include other abbreviations for techniques and instructions. These abbreviations may refer to specific actions, such as "yo" (yarn over) or "ch" (chain), or they may indicate special techniques, such as "inc" (increase) or "dec" (decrease). Understanding these abbreviations is crucial for following crochet patterns accurately and achieving the desired outcome.

Furthermore, it is important to note that crochet terms and abbreviations can vary slightly depending on the country or region. For example, in the United States, the double crochet stitch is often abbreviated as "dc," while in the United Kingdom, it is abbreviated as "tr." This slight variation can sometimes lead to confusion, especially when following patterns from different sources. Therefore, it is essential to familiarize oneself with the specific abbreviations used in the region or country where the pattern originates.

To grasp basic crochet terms and abbreviations, beginners can refer to various resources such as crochet books, online tutorials, and crochet communities. These resources often provide comprehensive lists of common crochet terms and abbreviations, along with detailed explanations and visual demonstrations. Additionally, practicing these terms and abbreviations through small projects or swatches can help solidify understanding and improve crochet skills

Techniques: Slip Knots, Chain Stitches, and Turning Your Work of Crochet: Crochet is a popular craft that involves creating fabric by interlocking loops of yarn or thread using a crochet hook. To get started with crochet, it is essential to learn some basic techniques such as slip knots, chain stitches, and turning your work.

The first technique, slip knots, is used to create a secure loop on your crochet hook. This loop serves as the foundation for your crochet project. To make a slip knot, start by creating a loop with the yarn, ensuring that the tail end of the yarn is on top. Insert your crochet hook through the loop and pull the yarn through, creating a new loop. Tighten the knot by pulling the tail end of the yarn gently. Slip knots are essential as they allow you to easily attach your yarn to the crochet hook and begin your project.

Once you have your slip knot ready, you can move on to the next technique, chain stitches. Chain stitches are the building blocks of crochet and are used to create a foundation row for your project. To make a chain stitch, insert your crochet hook into the slip knot loop and yarn over, which means wrapping the yarn around the hook. Pull the yarn through the loop on your hook, creating a new loop. Repeat this process until you have the desired number of chain stitches. Chain stitches are typically used to create a base for other crochet stitches and patterns.

After mastering slip knots and chain stitches, it is important to learn how to turn your work in crochet. Turning your work allows you to continue crocheting in the opposite direction, creating rows of stitches. To turn your work, simply rotate your crochet piece 180 degrees, so the side you were working on is now facing away from you. This allows you to work on the opposite side and create a symmetrical and balanced crochet project. Turning your work is crucial for creating various crochet patterns and designs.

In conclusion, slip knots, chain stitches, and turning your work are fundamental techniques in crochet. Mastering these techniques will provide you with a solid foundation to create beautiful and intricate crochet projects. Whether you are a beginner or an experienced crocheter, understanding these techniques is essential for expanding your crochet skills and exploring more complex patterns and designs. So grab your crochet hook, yarn, and start practicing these techniques to unleash your creativity and create stunning crochet masterpieces.

The Fundamental Crochet Stitches: Single, Double, and Half Double: Crochet is a popular craft that involves creating fabric by interlocking loops of yarn or thread using a crochet hook. There are several fundamental crochet stitches that form the basis of most crochet projects. These stitches include the single crochet, double crochet, and half double crochet.

The single crochet stitch is the most basic crochet stitch and is often the first stitch beginners learn. To create a single crochet stitch, you start by inserting the crochet hook into the next stitch, yarn over, and pull through a loop. Then, yarn over again and pull through both loops on the hook. This creates a single crochet stitch. Single crochet stitches are typically shorter and tighter than other crochet stitches, making them ideal for creating dense and sturdy fabric.

The double crochet stitch is slightly taller than the single crochet stitch and is commonly used in a variety of crochet projects. To create a double crochet stitch, you start by yarn over, then insert the crochet hook into the next stitch, yarn over again, and pull through a loop. Next, yarn over and pull through the first two loops on the hook, and then yarn over again and pull through the remaining two loops. This completes a double crochet stitch. Double crochet stitches are often used to create more open and lacy fabric, as they are taller and looser than single crochet stitches.

The half double crochet stitch is a versatile stitch that falls in between the height of a single crochet and a double crochet stitch. To create a half double crochet stitch, you start by yarn over, then insert the crochet hook into the next stitch, yarn over again, and pull through a loop. Next, yarn over and pull through all three loops on the hook. This completes a half double crochet stitch. Half double crochet stitches are often used to create fabric with a medium thickness and drape, making them suitable for a wide range of crochet projects.

These fundamental crochet stitches can be combined and manipulated in various ways to create intricate patterns and designs. By mastering these stitches, crocheters can create a wide range of items, from simple scarves and blankets to more complex garments and accessories. Additionally, these stitches can be used in combination with other crochet techniques, such as increases and decreases, to shape the fabric and create different textures.

In conclusion, the single crochet, double crochet, and half double crochet stitches are the foundation of crochet. Each stitch has its own unique characteristics and uses, allowing crocheters to create a variety of fabric textures and designs.

Introducing Textured Stitches: Bobble, Cluster, and Popcorn of Crochet:

Crochet is a versatile and creative craft that allows you to create beautiful and intricate designs using just a hook and yarn. One of the most exciting aspects of crochet is the ability to incorporate various stitches and techniques to add texture and dimension to your projects. Among these textured stitches, the bobble, cluster, and popcorn stitches stand out as popular choices for adding depth and interest to your crochet creations.

The bobble stitch is a fun and playful stitch that creates small, raised bumps on your fabric. It is achieved by working multiple stitches into the same stitch or space and then closing them together to form a cluster. This creates a rounded, three-dimensional effect that adds a unique texture to your crochet work. Bobble stitches can be used to create a variety of patterns, from simple polka dots to more intricate designs like flowers or animal motifs. They can be worked in a single color or combined with other stitches to create stunning colorwork effects.

The cluster stitch is another textured stitch that is commonly used in crochet. It involves working multiple stitches together into the same stitch or space, similar to the bobble stitch. However, unlike the bobble stitch, the cluster stitch is usually worked over a larger number of stitches, resulting in a more elongated and less rounded texture. Cluster stitches can be used to create a wide range of patterns, from simple stripes to more complex lace designs. They can also be combined with other stitches to create interesting textures and patterns.

The popcorn stitch is a unique and eye-catching stitch that creates small, puffy balls on your fabric. It is achieved by working multiple stitches into the same stitch or space and then closing them together to form a cluster. However, unlike the bobble and cluster stitches, the popcorn stitch is not closed together, resulting in a more pronounced and raised texture. Popcorn stitches can be used to create a variety of patterns, from simple polka dots to more intricate designs like flowers or geometric shapes. They can be worked in a single color or combined with other stitches to create stunning colorwork effects.

These textured stitches, including the bobble, cluster, and popcorn stitches, offer endless possibilities for adding depth and interest to your crochet projects. Whether you're creating a cozy blanket, a stylish sweater, or a cute amigurumi toy, incorporating these stitches can take your crochet work to the next level.

Working in the Round: Making Circles and Tubes of Crochet:

Crocheting in the round is a technique that allows you to create circles and tubes without the need for seams. It is a versatile and essential skill for any crocheter, as it can be used to make a wide range of projects such as hats, bags, amigurumi, and even blankets.

To start working in the round, you will need a crochet hook and yarn of your choice. It is important to choose a hook size that matches the weight of your yarn to ensure that your stitches are even and the finished project has the desired drape.

There are two main methods for starting a round: the magic ring and the chain ring. The magic ring is a popular technique that creates a tight and adjustable center for your project. It involves creating a loop with your yarn, inserting the hook through the loop, and then working your first round of stitches into the loop. The chain ring method involves creating a chain of stitches and then joining the last stitch to the first stitch with a slip stitch to form a ring.

Once you have established your starting point, you will continue working in a spiral, without turning your work. This means that you will be working in a continuous circle, rather than in rows. To create a circle, you will need to increase the number of stitches in each round. This can be done by working multiple stitches into the same stitch or by working an increase stitch, such as a double crochet increase or a half double crochet increase.

To create a tube, you will need to maintain the same number of stitches in each round. This can be achieved by working a consistent number of stitches in each round, without any increases or decreases. Tubes are commonly used for projects such as sleeves, leg warmers, and the bodies of amigurumi.

When working in the round, it is important to keep track of your rounds. This can be done by using stitch markers or by counting your stitches at the end of each round. It is also helpful to use a stitch marker to mark the beginning of each round, as this will make it easier to keep track of where you are in your project.

Working in the round can be a bit challenging at first, especially if you are used to working in rows. However, with practice and patience, it becomes a natural and enjoyable technique.

Increasing and Decreasing: Giving Shape to Your Projects of Crochet: The input this book suggests a topic related to the techniques of increasing and decreasing in crochet, which are essential for creating various shapes and dimensions in crochet projects. This topic is of great importance to crochet enthusiasts, as it allows them to add depth, texture, and structure to their creations.

Crochet, a versatile and popular craft, involves creating fabric by interlocking loops of yarn using a crochet hook. While the basic stitches like single crochet, double crochet, and treble crochet are commonly used, the techniques of increasing and decreasing take crochet to a whole new level by enabling the creation of intricate patterns and three-dimensional shapes.

Increasing in crochet refers to adding stitches to the existing row or round, resulting in a wider or larger piece of fabric. This technique is often used to create flared edges, ruffles, or to shape garments such as sleeves, hats, or skirts. There are various methods of increasing in crochet, including the simple increase, where two stitches are worked into the same stitch, and the chain increase, where additional chains are made before working into the next stitch. Understanding and mastering these techniques is crucial for achieving the desired shape and size in crochet projects.

On the other hand, decreasing in crochet involves reducing the number of stitches in a row or round, resulting in a narrower or smaller piece of fabric. This technique is commonly used to shape garments, amigurumi toys, or other crochet items that require a tapered or fitted look. Decreasing can be achieved through techniques such as single crochet decrease, double crochet decrease, or slip stitch decrease. Each method creates a different effect and it is important to choose the appropriate one based on the desired outcome.

By combining increasing and decreasing techniques, crocheters can create a wide range of shapes and dimensions in their projects. For example, by increasing gradually at the beginning and decreasing gradually towards the end, one can create a triangular shawl or a trapezoid-shaped bag. Similarly, by strategically increasing and decreasing in specific areas, intricate patterns such as chevrons, shells, or waves can be achieved.

Understanding the principles of increasing and decreasing in crochet not only allows for more creative freedom but also ensures that the finished project has a professional and polished look. It is important to practice these techniques and experiment with different stitch combinations to gain confidence and proficiency in shaping crochet projects.

The Basics of Changing Colors in Crochet: Changing colors in crochet is a fundamental technique that allows you to create beautiful and intricate designs in your projects. Whether you're a beginner or an experienced crocheter, understanding the basics of changing colors will open up a world of possibilities for you.

To start, you'll need two or more colors of yarn. It's important to choose colors that complement each other and create the desired effect in your project. You can either use different shades of the same color or contrasting colors for a more vibrant look.

When you're ready to change colors, there are a few different methods you can use. One common method is the cut and tie method, where you simply cut the yarn of the old color, leaving a tail, and tie on the new color. This method is quick and easy, but it can result in a lot of loose ends to weave in later.

Another method is the "carry along" method, where you carry the unused color along the back of your work as you crochet with the new color. This method is great for projects with small color changes or when you want to minimize the number of loose ends. However, it can be a bit trickier to keep the carried yarn neat and tidy.

To change colors using the cut and tie method, follow these steps:

1. When you reach the last stitch of the old color, stop before completing the stitch.

2. Cut the yarn of the old color, leaving a tail of about 6 inches.

3. Take the new color and make a slipknot on your hook.

4. Insert your hook into the last stitch of the old color and pull the new color through.

5. Complete the stitch with the new color, securing the tail of the old color as you go.

6. Continue crocheting with the new color, leaving the tail of the old color hanging.

7. Later, you can weave in the loose ends using a yarn needle to secure them and prevent unraveling.

When changing colors using the carry along method, follow these steps:

1. When you're ready to change colors, stop before completing the last stitch of the old color.

2. Drop the old color and pick up the new color, leaving a tail of about 6 inches.

3. Insert your hook into the last stitch of the old color and pull the new color through.

4. Continue crocheting with the new color, carrying the old color along the back of your work.

Reading and Deciphering Crochet Patterns: Reading and deciphering crochet patterns can be a challenging task, especially for beginners. However, with practice and a good understanding of the symbols and abbreviations used in crochet patterns, it becomes easier to follow and create beautiful crochet projects.

When you first look at a crochet pattern, it may seem like a foreign language with its combination of letters, numbers, and symbols. However, each element in the pattern has a specific meaning and purpose, and once you learn to decode them, you'll be able to create intricate and stunning crochet designs.

One of the first things you'll notice in a crochet pattern is the list of materials needed. This includes the type and weight of yarn, the recommended hook size, and any additional tools or accessories required. It's important to pay attention to these details as they can greatly affect the outcome of your project.

Next, you'll come across the gauge or tension information. This tells you how many stitches and rows should be worked in a specific measurement, usually 4 inches or 10 centimeters. Following the gauge is crucial to ensure that your finished project matches the size and shape specified in the pattern.

The pattern itself is usually written in a combination of abbreviations and symbols. Each stitch has its own abbreviation, such as "sc" for single crochet or "dc" for double crochet. These abbreviations are commonly used in crochet patterns to save space and make the instructions more concise.

In addition to abbreviations, crochet patterns also use symbols to represent different stitches and techniques. These symbols are often included in a chart or diagram, which provides a visual representation of the pattern. Learning to read crochet charts can be extremely helpful, especially for complex patterns or when working with international patterns that may use different abbreviations.

As you read through the pattern, you'll also encounter instructions for special stitches or techniques. These may include increases, decreases, or specific stitch combinations that create unique textures or patterns. It's important to carefully read and understand these instructions before attempting them, as they can greatly impact the overall look and structure of your crochet project.

To successfully decipher a crochet pattern, it's essential to have a good understanding of basic crochet stitches and techniques. If you're a beginner, it's recommended to start with simple patterns that use basic stitches like single crochet or double crochet. As you gain more experience and confidence, you can gradually move on to more complex patterns that incorporate advanced stitches and techniques.

Simple Guidelines for Designing Your Own Patterns of Crochet:

Designing your own crochet patterns can be a rewarding and creative experience. It allows you to express your unique style and create one-of-a-kind pieces. However, it can also be a daunting task if you're not sure where to start. That's why we've put together these simple guidelines to help you get started on your journey of designing your own crochet patterns.

1. Choose your inspiration: Before you begin designing, it's important to have a clear idea of what you want to create. Look for inspiration in various sources such as nature, fashion, or even other crochet patterns. Take note of the colors, textures, and shapes that catch your eye. This will help you create a cohesive and visually appealing design.

2. Sketch your ideas: Once you have your inspiration, start sketching your ideas on paper. This will give you a visual representation of your design and help you plan out the details. Don't worry about being an artist – a simple sketch will do. Focus on capturing the overall shape and structure of your design.

3. Choose your yarn and hook: The choice of yarn and hook size will greatly impact the final outcome of your design. Consider the drape, texture, and weight you want for your finished piece. Experiment with different yarns and hooks to find the perfect combination that brings your design to life.

4. Start with a swatch: Before diving into your full design, it's always a good idea to create a swatch. This will help you determine the gauge and ensure that your finished piece will have the desired measurements. It's also an opportunity to test different stitch patterns and see how they work together.

5. Plan your stitch pattern: Once you have your swatch, it's time to plan your stitch pattern. Consider the overall structure of your design and how different stitches can create the desired effect. Experiment with different stitch combinations, textures, and color changes to add depth and interest to your design.

6. Create a written pattern: As you work on your design, make sure to keep track of your stitches and rows. This will help you create a written pattern that others can follow. Include clear instructions, abbreviations, and any special techniques used. A well-written pattern will make it easier for others to recreate your design.

7. Test and adjust: Once you have your written pattern, it's important to test it out. Crochet your design following the instructions and make note

INTRODUCTION

If you're trying to seek out easy to follow beginner crochet lessons, fun and unique patterns and useful tips, stop and check no further because you came to the right place. All of those things are right here during this book and expecting you to form use of.

All of the teachings during this book are easy to follow and that they are beat an order that creates sense to the beginner.

The lessons accompany clear written instructions, and each one among the instructions have clear, bright, and colorful pictures.

All of the patterns that I demonstrate here during this book accompany helpful pictures, abbreviation guides, and stitch explanations. I also plan to add extra side note descriptions so as that everything in my patterns are made more clear.

The lessons during this book accompany helpful and more importantly useful tips. I attempt to make each tip important, and their job is to feature value to your learning experience. When there's something that needs clarification during a lesson, that's where I usually see the necessity to put a tip. the ideas in each lesson really do make it easier to seek out crochet.

If you'd wish to seek out the way to crochet, then begin your journey here!

Follow my easy to use step-by-step directions and get to find out great crochet instructions every beginner should have.

CHAPTER 1

The Crochet Supplies You Need to Start Up

In the event that you are an amateur to crochet and need to realize which crochet supplies are important to begin, you are at the correct spot.

In the event that you are befuddled by the entirety of the yarn and crochet hook decisions being sold in stores, this exercise will remove the mystery from what to buy.

The incredible thing about crochet is its moderateness. The main supplies you have to begin are the correct crochet hook, an amateur yarn and some scissors made for crochet.

Audit of Supplies

1. Crochet Hook

The best crochet hook to buy when first figuring out how to crochet is a size I-9 hook. Presently many feel that a size H-8 crochet hook is ideal, yet I suggest an I-9 hook in light of the solace it gives and the greater lines it makes.

Try not to begin with a plastic or a wooden hook in light of the fact that the yarn doesn't float well over these sorts of hooks. Be that as it may, these kinds of hooks are phenomenal for further developed crocheters.

Do begin with an aluminum hook. This sort of hook is incredible for tenderfoots and is entirely moderate!

 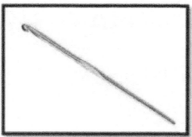

2. Yarn

Having the right crochet supplies is significant, and yarn is an absolute necessity. Pick a yarn that is strong in tincture, and ensure you avoid a diverse yarn in light of the fact that the lines will be extremely hard to separate when first figuring out how to knit.

Pick a colour that is light or splendid in shading. Again you need to have the option to see your fastens.

Buy a worsted weight yarn made of acrylic or fleece filaments. There ought to be an image of the number four on the mark on the off chance that you are uncertain.

Any brand of yarn ought to be fine, yet on the off chance that you are as yet uncertain what to purchase go out and buy Red Heart. This is a truly moderate yarn and it is anything but difficult to work with.

3. Pair of Scissors

Buy some scissors that are little and have a sharp point. This kind of scissor is made for crafts like crochet.

Tip: The crochet hook, yarn and pair of scissors just talked about in this chapter are supplies implied for the novice.

There will be more crochet materials you will need to add to your assortment sometime in the not too distant future, yet for the present, these things will make you knit like a genius instantly.

Yarn

Scissors

CHAPTER 2

Figure out how to Hold a Crochet Hook

In all honesty, when figuring out how to hold a crochet hook, you're the person who chooses which strategy is best for you and your solace!

Presently in light of saying that keep there are a few strategies for holding a hook, and I am going to show the two most famous methods of doing as such before you choose which procedure works best for you.

Presently on the off chance that you wind up holding your hook somewhat better than the two techniques appeared in this exercise, try not to be reluctant to simply go with it!

Holding a Crochet Hook Review

Before you figure out how to hold a crochet hook, the principal thing you need to know is the place the hook's handle and thumb-rest (found in outline beneath) are found. Along these lines when I talk about hook position you won't be totally lost.

In the outline underneath, I additionally call attention to the hook's pole, point and throat just in the event that you are intrigued!

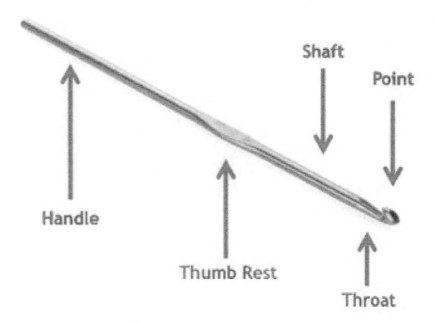

Tip: I trust I am not expressing the self-evident, however just in the event that you didn't definitely realize; the crochet hook is set in your prevailing hand.

Methods of Holding a Crochet Hook

There are two basic methods of holding a crochet hook. These include:

1. Knife Method:

As the name implies, here the crochet hook is held precisely the same way the knife is held while eating.

Ensure your thumb and center finger are getting a handle on the thumb-rest and the crochet hook's handle is leaning against your palm.

Look beneath at some engaging pictures of how to hold your hook utilizing the knife strategy - I trust they are engaging at any rate!

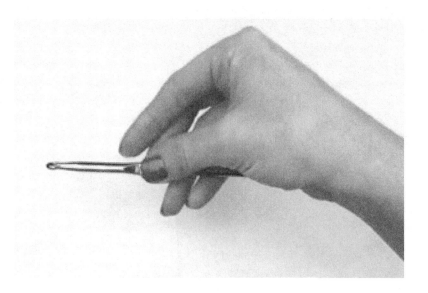

2. Fork Method:

This strategy is likewise called the pencil technique; however, I for one like any phrasing that manages food much better.

Hold your crochet hook a similar way you hold your fork while eating.

Ensure your thumb and index finger are complaining the thumb-rest, and the handle is laying on the meaty zone over your pointer.

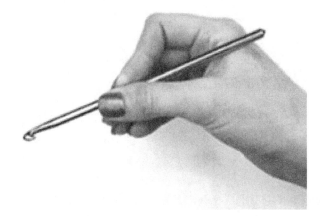

Tip: When first figuring out how to hold a crochet hook, your hands can get confined on the off chance that you don't have the correct grasp. So continue changing and attempt various strategies until the hook feels directly in your grasp.

Recollect there is no set standard to holding a hook and you truly need to discover what works for you.

CHAPTER 3

Step by Step Instructions to Hold Yarn for Crochet

On the off chance that you are thinking about how to hold yarn for crochet, the principal rule is there are no guidelines! So to put it plainly, do whatever feels right when holding your yarn.

Presently I understand that you most likely have never crocheted, and if so, permit me to give you some famous strategies before you choose what direction is best for you.

Holding Yarn Review

Here are a couple of tips before beginning:

The yarn is put in your less predominant hand.

The yarn hand takes care of the yarn to your hook while you knit, and this is the reason it is imperative to discover a holding style that works best for you with the goal that you are agreeable while crocheting.

The yarn hand controls the pressure of the yarn being taken care of, and decides how close or free your completed undertaking will be.

This may not bode well right now, however once you really begin crocheting, these tips will turn out to be all the more clear.

Methods

Side Note: While I show you how to hold yarn for crochet, I like to give names for the diverse yarn holding methods that I illustrate.

So uncovered as a main priority the names I have made for the methods utilized are not regularly utilized for stitch phrasing purposes.

1. The Pinky Hold Technique

The little finger (pinky) does a large portion of the work in this technique.

Stage 1: With palm looking down, bring the last part of your yarn up between your little finger and ring finger. (Showing underneath)

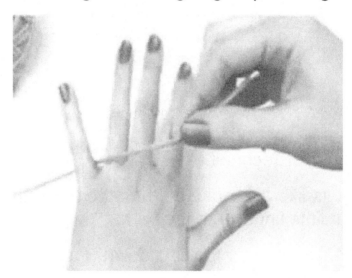

Stage 2: Wrap the last part of your yarn around your little finger shaping a circle around your pinky finger.

Stage 3: Bring the last part of the yarn over the head of your hand.

Stage 4: Allow your thumb and index finger to hold the yarn for control.

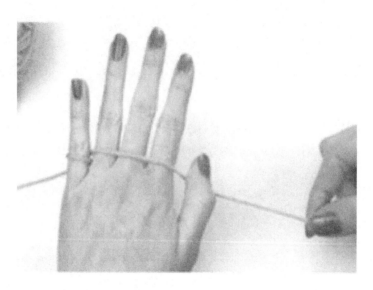

2. The Loose Yarn Technique

This strategy is like the pinky hold method, however this time you won't wrap your little finger with the yarn.

Stage 1: With your palm looking down, force the last part of the yarn up through, and in the middle of your little finger and ring finger.

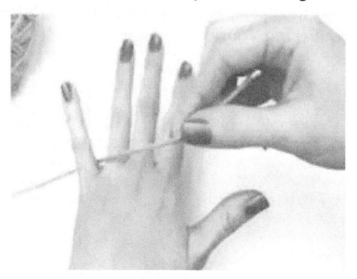

Stage 2: Continue to pull the yarn over the head of your hand getting it with your thumb and pointer for control.

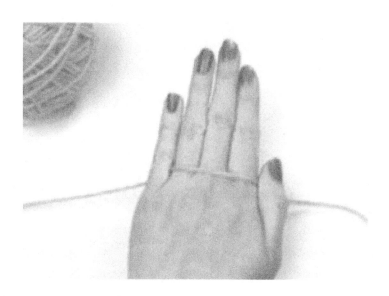

3. The Forefinger Hold Technique

In this procedure, the pointer (forefinger) will do the greater part of the work for you.

Stage 1: With palm looking down, bring the last part of the yarn up through your little finger and forefinger.

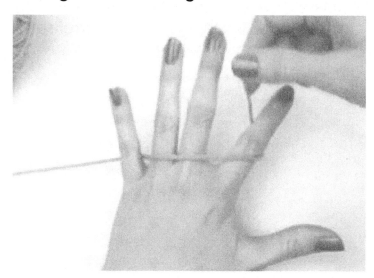

Stage 2: Continue to bring the yarn over the head of your hand circling it around your pointer (forefinger).

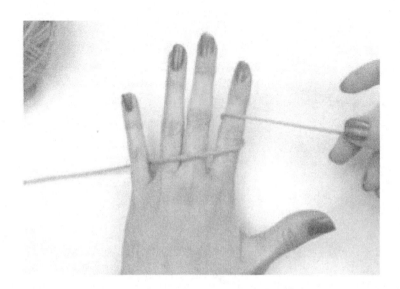

On the off chance that you concoct your own strategy when figuring out how to hold yarn for stitch that works as well, begin by utilizing the strategies that I have demonstrated you as a rule, and afterward sever and have a go at something else.

Tip: The significant thing to recall is to consistently be agreeable while knitting. On the off chance that your hand begins to seize up when you are utilizing a specific style, quit utilizing that style and have a go at something other than what's expected.

CHAPTER 4

Make a Crochet Slip Knot

A knit slip hitch is imperative to ace since it is the initial step taken when starting any knitted piece.

At the point when you choose to knit a basic dishcloth or an intricate outfit, a slip bunch will be your beginning stage.

There are a few varieties someone crocheting can utilize when making a slip tie, and in this chapter I will show three generally utilized procedures since everybody's style is unique.

Here are a couple of tips before beginning:

Start your slip hitch by pulling 6 to 8 creeps of yarn from the skein (wad of yarn).

The working finish of yarn originates from the skein, and the last part of yarn is the yarn being utilized or worked. (Representation beneath)

In the event that you stall out or hate any strategy being appeared, proceed onward to the following method and discover something that works for you!

The names utilized for these strategies are names that I have compensated for showing purposes and not viewed as a piece of sew wording.

Working end of yarn

Tail end

1. The Pretzel Technique

I call this the pretzel strategy since you shape the yarn into a pretzel before making your knit slip hitch.

Stage 1: Take the last part of yarn and circle it over the working finish of yarn.

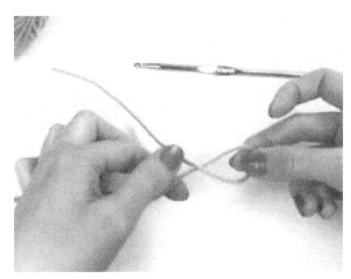

Stage 2: Pull and crease the last part of the yarn rearward of the circle making a pretzel shape.

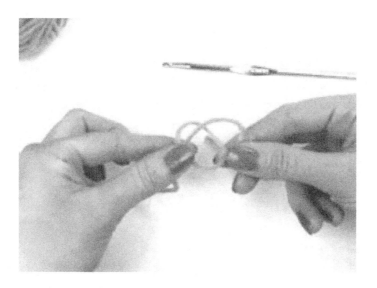

Stage 3: Insert your hook through the main circle of the pretzel.

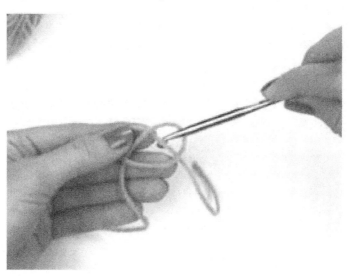

Stage 4: Pull the circle through the pretzel making your sew slip tie.

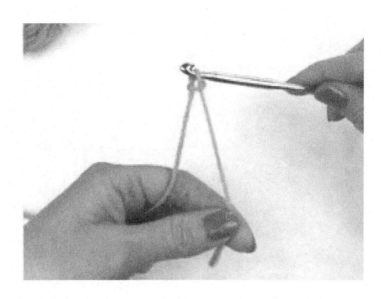

2. The "X" Technique

I call this the X procedure since you shape the yarn into an X shape before making your slip tie.

Stage 1: Take the last part of your yarn and fold it over your list and center fingers.

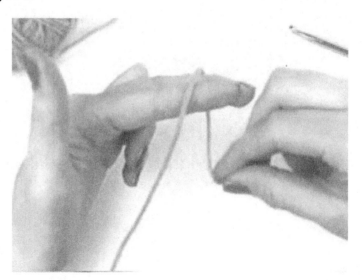

Stage 2: Continue to cross the last part of your yarn over the head of your fingers again making the letter X.

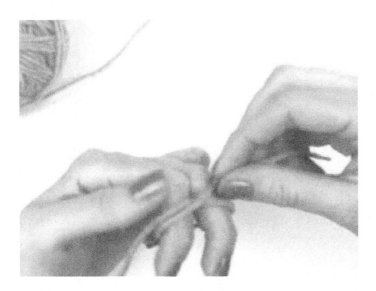

Stage 3: Push the yarn through the main circle being mindful so as not to drive excessively far causing the whole last part to come through.

Stage 4: Pull your center and forefinger out of the X circle and get the working and last part of yarn. Fix to make you knit slip tie.

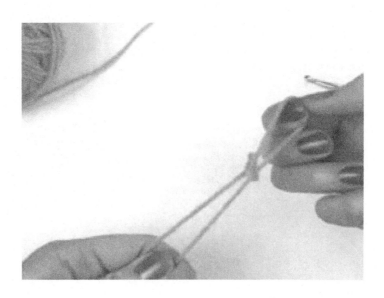

3. The Flip Technique

Stage 1: Take the last part of the yarn and circle it over the working finish of the yarn. Do this by holding the yarn or laying it on a level surface.

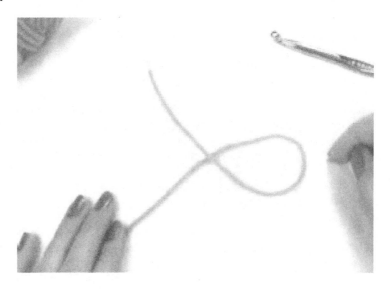

Stage 2: Pull the circle and flip it over the working finish of the yarn.

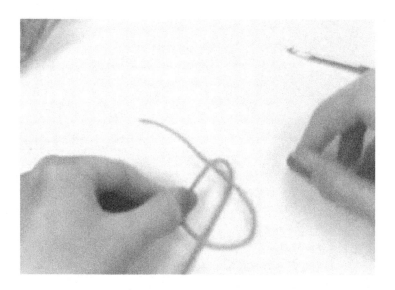

Stage 3: Place hook in predominant hand and slid it under the working strand of the yarn that is under the circle.

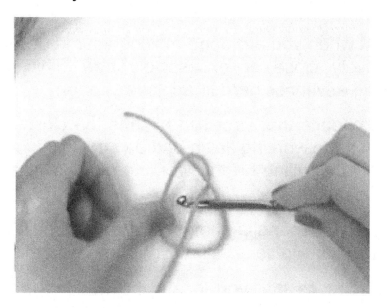

Stage 4: Pull the working finish of the yarn through the circle with your knit hook and this will make your slip knot.

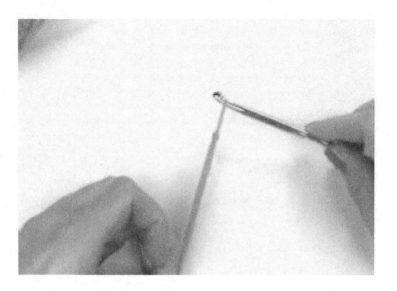

Here are some useful hints on the off chance that you are as yet experiencing difficulty

At the point when you are done making your knot slip tie, ensure it isn't excessively close or excessively free. This will make the accompanying advances hard to achieve later on.

On the off chance that your slip hitch is too close utilize a bigger hook, or pull on the working finish of the yarn while your slip tie is still on your hook. By pulling on the working finish of the yarn your slip bunch will release up.

In the event that your slip knot is too free, draw on the last part of the yarn while your slip tie is still on your hook and this will fix it up.

On the off chance that you locate the working finish of the yarn fixing as opposed to slackening, and the last part relaxing as opposed to fixing your slip tie don't stress over it!

CHAPTER 5

Get Familiar with The Crochet Chain

At the point when you're new to knitting, the crochet chain is the principal join you have to realize when beginning your absolute first undertaking.

The explanation behind this is on the grounds that the chain fastening is the establishment for crochet, and pretty much every example starts with a chain line.

Indeed, the chain, or chain fasten is in fact called an establishment chain, albeit numerous novices to crochet don't understand this yet!

However, since you know the word establishment chain is the right crochet phrasing, you will presently have the option to recognize what examples and individual crochet companions are discussing later on!

Step by step instructions to make the Crochet Chain (Establishment Chain)

The Procedures:

Stage 1: Make a slip hitch. (See Chapter 4 "Make a Crochet Slip Knot" for additional consideration of the slip hitch)

Stage 2: Place the slip tie onto the hook.

The image underneath is indicating Step 2: The slip tie position on the hook.

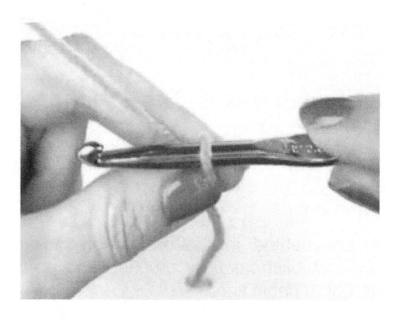

Stage 3: Yarn Over. Yarn over is a term all crocheters use, and it is a significant term to know since it is the main development you make to the yarn with your hook before making any sort of crochet fasten - this incorporates the crochet chain.

The most effective method to Yarn Over

Yarn Over is straightforward: All you do is fold the yarn around your hook from back to front, or at the end of the day, drive the yarn away from your hook before seizing it with the hook's throat.

Yarn Over is abridged (YO). This will turn out to be more essential to you when you begin understanding examples.

The Picture underneath is indicating Stage 3 (What yarn over resembles).

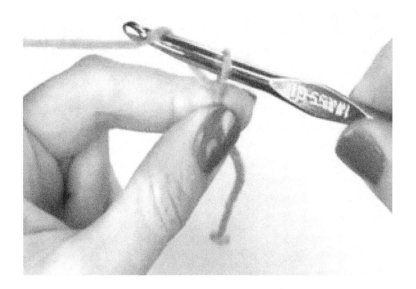

Stage 4: Rotate the hook until it is looking down, or toward the slip tie.

The image underneath is indicating Stage 4 (Rotate the hook down).

Stage 5: Pull the yarn through the circle the on your hook, and this makes the primary chain.

Chain is truncated (CH). Again this will turn out to be more significant when you start understanding examples.

The photos beneath show Stage 5 (Pull the yarn through the circle).

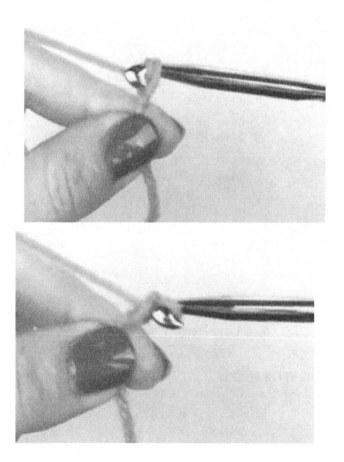

To make more chains, proceed with this procedure by utilizing the yarn over, and get through the circle methods. Prop up until your ideal chain length is practiced.

Affixing Tips

Tip 1: As the stitch chain (establishment chain) gets longer, keep on moving your fingers up the chain to keep control.

Tip 2: Each chain ought to be a similar size, so ensure your strain on the yarn is the equivalent for each chain you make.

Tip 3: If your fastens are tight and you find that you can't get the hook through the join, you have to loosen up your hands more.

Tip 4: If your joins are free, ensure your hold on the yarn and hook is minimal more tight... you may likewise need to bring your yarn hand and hook hand nearer together to abbreviate the separation between two hands.

Checking Chain Stitches

At the point when you have completed your chain, you may not be certain what number of chain fastens you've quite recently made.

Start by checking the main fasten that is directly underneath the circle on your hook, and proceed by tallying the "V" molded join right to the start of your chain.

Here is a Tip for Counting Stitches:

Never tally the circle that is still on your hook when checking your join, and never tally the slip hitch.

CHAPTER 6

The Single Crochet Stitch

The single crochet fasten is viewed as the most usually utilized join in stitch. So it bodes well that you ought to get familiar with this line first.

Single crochet is curtailed (SC) - Important to know for design perusing.

Look down for point by point composed guidelines on the most proficient method to single stitch.

Instructions to do the Single Crochet Stitch

Procedures for Single Crochet:

Stage 1: Make an establishment chain by fastening 30 lines (CH 30).

See image of Stage 1, establishment chain underneath.

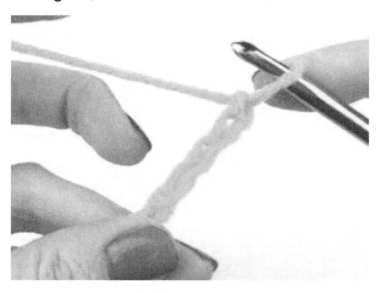

Stage 2: Insert your crochet hook into the second chain from the hook. Ensure you embed your guide into the top circle as it were.

There should now be two circles on your hook.

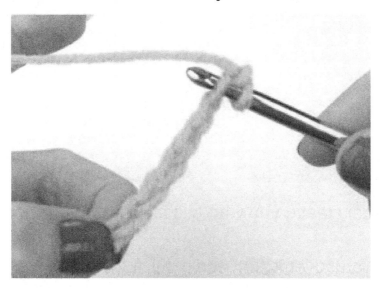

Stage 3: Yarn over (YO) your hook. Do this by folding the yarn around your hook from back to front, or at the end of the day push the hook under the yarn strand, and afterward rotate the yarn toward you until the hook is looking down.

The yarn should now be on the hook's throat

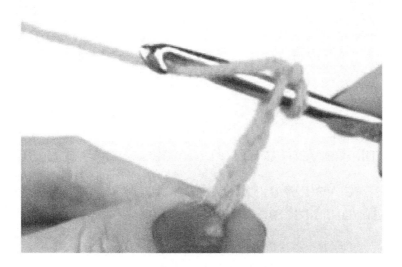

Stage 4: Pull the yarn through the principal circle on your hook.

This will again leave you with two circles on your hook.

Stage 5: Yarn over (YO) again by folding the yarn around your hook again.

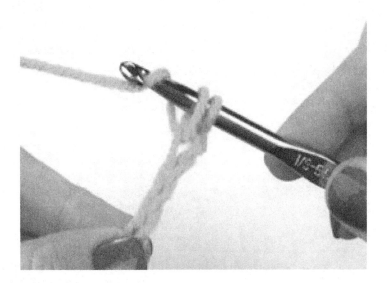

Stage 6: Pull the yarn through the two circles on your hook.

This will leave you with one strand of yarn on your hook, and will likewise finish your first single crochet join (SC)!

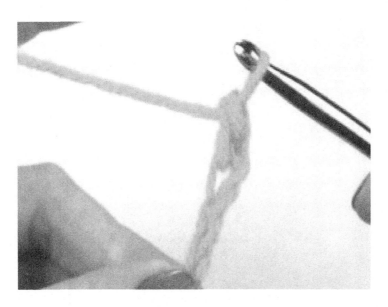

Make a point to proceed with this identical join design all through your whole chain.

When you are done you ought to have (29 SC) in succession.

Tip: If you are pondering where join 30 went, simply recollect that you skirted the principal chain on your hook, with the goal that implies just 29 single crochet (SC) are expected to finish the line.

This is what your single crochet line ought to resemble when it is done.

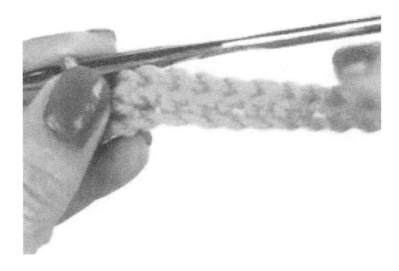

Instructions to Single Crochet into the Next Row

Stage 1: Chain 1 (CH 1).

Recall when you chain you yarn over and afterward get through the circle on the hook.

There should now be one circle on your hook.

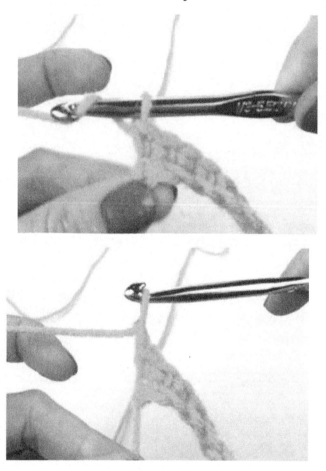

Stage 2: Bring your work toward you and get it turned.

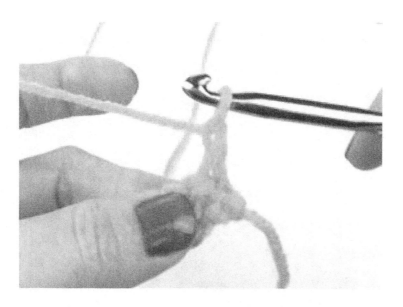

Stage 3: Insert your hook into the primary single crochet join.

Tip: The head of the line on a solitary stitch resembles the letter "V", and this is the place you need to embed your hook.

There will currently be three circles on your hook in light of the fact that the (SC) line is comprised of two circles.

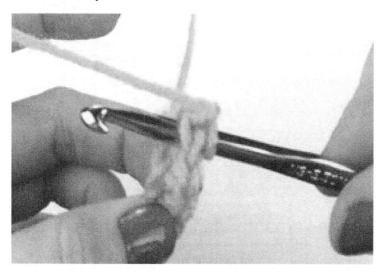

Stage 4: Yarn over (YO).

Stage 5: Pull the yarn through the line on your hook.

This implies you should just get the yarn through the initial two circles on your hook. Recall the initial two circles make up the single sew fasten.

There should now be two circles on your hook.

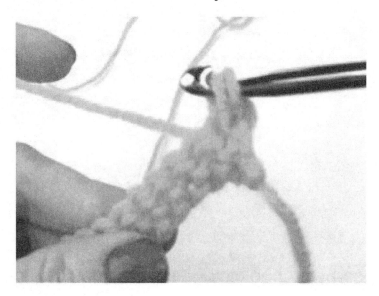

Stage 6: Yarn over (YO).

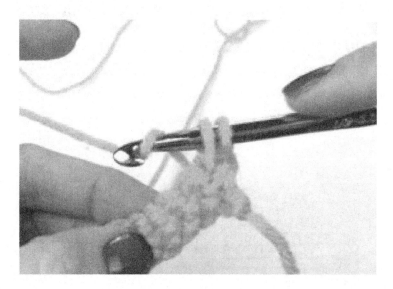

Stage 7: Pull the yarn through the two circles on your hook.

There will presently be one circle left on your hook, and your first single crochet is done.

Feel free to complete this column by finishing stages 1to 7. Take on a third row before moving on to the next exercise.

CHAPTER 7

Figure out How to Change Color in Crochet

Continuously recall, at the point when you change colour in crochet toward the start or end of a column you never need to tie off, or place a slip hitch anyplace in your venture.

Changing yarn colour is a lot simpler than you understand, and this chapter will give you how it's finished!!!

Look down for composed guidelines on the best way to change yarn shading.

The most effective method to Change Color in Crochet

Tip: I am utilizing the single crochet line in this show, however recollect the rules are the equivalent for any crochet fasten that you use.

Stage 1: When changing colour toward the start or end of a line, you never need to finish the last fasten. Rather you will need to work your last fasten to the last two circles on your hook. Recollect this goes for some other fasten utilized too!

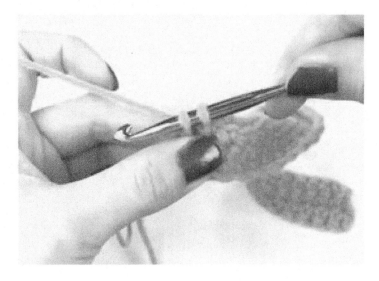

Stage 2: Fold the new yarn colour fifty-fifty by leaving 4 to 5 creeps of yarn on the last part.

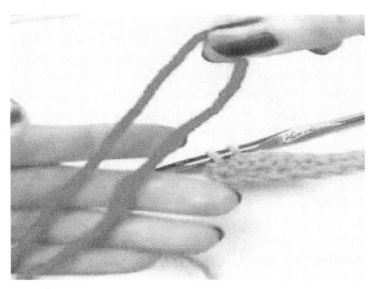

Stage 3: Pinch the two closures together at the top by utilizing your thumb and pointer.

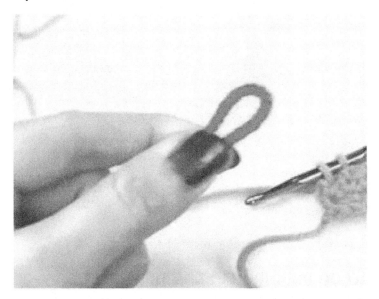

Stage 4: Place the new yarn on your hook and get the new colour through the two circles on your hook.

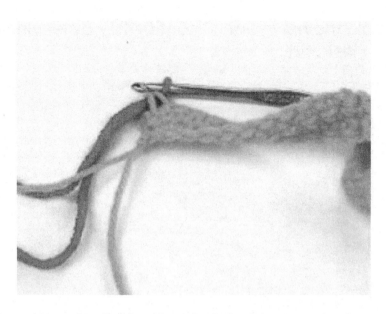

Stage 5: Cut the principal colour's joined strand of yarn leaving 4 to 5 crawls of yarn appended.

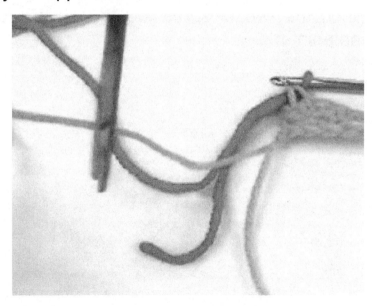

Stage 6: Pull on both the old and new last parts, or free strands of yarn to make sure about the new colour into place.

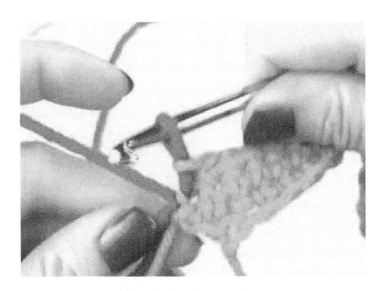

Stage 7: Chain 1 with the new colour.

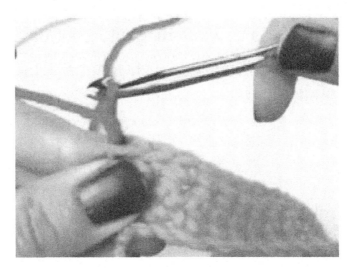

Stage 8: Turn your work around and hold the free strands together at the rear of your work. Presently knit over the two free strands 4 to multiple times before cutting the free strands with your scissors.

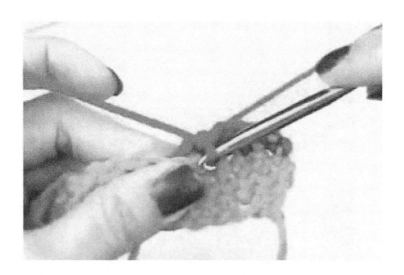

Rehash this procedure when you change to another colour.

In the event that you are tracking with this lesson, place four additional columns of the new shading into your dishcloth.

After you place the new lines, finish stages 1 to 8 and change to another colour once more.

CHAPTER 8

How to Finish a Crochet Venture the Correct Way

This exercise will show you the significance on the most proficient method to complete a stitch venture. So in the event that you are considering how to manage your free yarn closes since you are done with your work, follow the following two exercises to discover how.

Completing a knit task will be perhaps the least demanding exercise that you will follow in this arrangement in light of the fact that there is just one activity that you have to finish.

The main concern: Make sure you leave enough yarn toward the finish of your task for weaving in.

This implies when you are done with your venture and you are prepared to make the primary cut. It would be ideal if you ensure you leave at any rate 4 to 6 creeps of yarn left onto your task for weaving.

Picture = Stage 1: Leave in any event 4 to 6 crawls of yarn and at that point make your cut with the scissors.

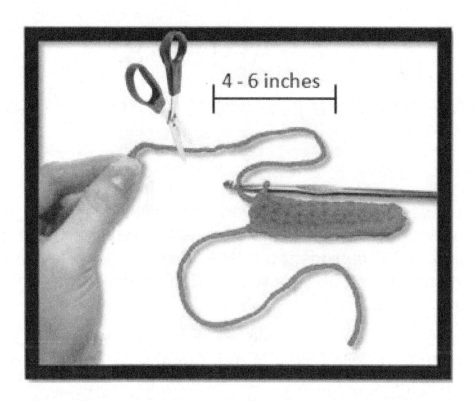

In the event that you don't have 4-6 crawls of yarn after your cut, you will wind up with a little strand of yarn standing out of your work and you won't have the option to weave it shut. Furthermore, you will be dismal with the completed outcomes.

Tip: With that said, it is additionally critical to begin your venture with a 4 to 6-inch strand of yarn too. This implies before you make your first slip tie when beginning your venture, get ready to leave 4-6 creeps of yarn standing out of the bunch. This will likewise be utilized for weaving toward the finish of your venture.

After you make your completing slice, all you have to do now is utilize your crochet hook to pull the remaining detail of yarn entirely through the last loop circle that is on your hook. Pull the yarn strand tight with your fingers and that is everything to this exercise!

Picture = Stage 2: Use the stitch hook to pull the remaining detail of yarn right through the keep going circle on the hook.

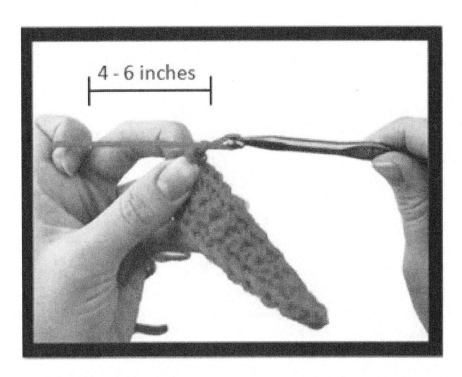

Picture = Stage 3: Pull the yarn strand tight with your fingers.

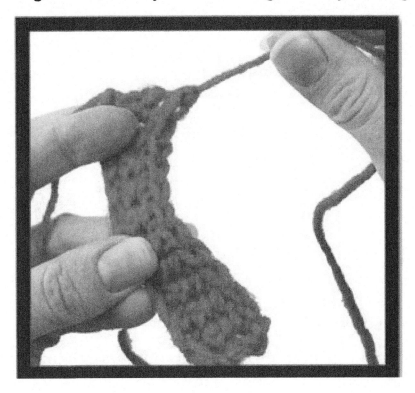

CHAPTER 9

Weaving in Yarn Ends

Figure out how to weave in yarn ends with the goal that your completed crochet venture looks stupendous!

In the event that you are stressed over your crochet venture disentangling, or in case you're similar to me and loathe taking a gander at those last parts of yarn standing out of your work, Look down for the bit by bit composed instructional exercise and you will perceive that it is so natural to shroud your free yarn finishes and make your task last!

Add a Yarn Needle to Your Crochet Supplies!

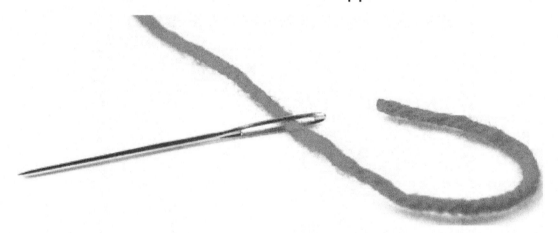

This is the ideal opportunity to add a yarn needle to your crochet kit. A yarn needle is a needle with a major eye and a dull point. It is perfect for weaving in yarn and makes an extraordinary expansion to your crochet supplies.

On the off chance that you don't have the needle right now there is no compelling reason to stress. Simply go out and get one when you can.

For the time being, simply utilize your crochet hook, yet make a point to weave the last parts of yarn in and out, and to and fro all through your task. You figure out how to do this with the composed instructional exercise (beneath). This will guarantee that those yarn ends won't begin standing out once more.

When working with the yarn needle, weave the last part of yarn all through your task. In addition to the fact that you want to zigzag all around the stitches, yet in addition make a point to weave to and fro all through similar fastens. This will help shield those closures from falling retreat.

Picture = Stage 1: Weave the yarn ends through the lines on the head of your venture.

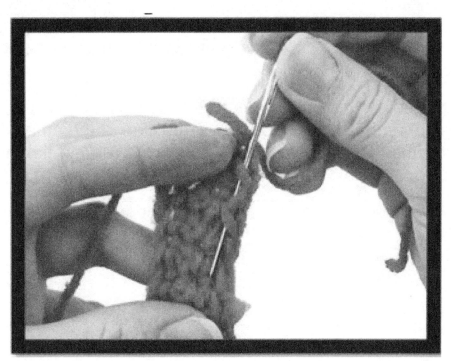

Picture = Stage 2: Weave the yarn ends through the center of your undertaking for a safer hold.

Tip: Free yarn ends can be weaved through the whole line. However, another incredible method to do this is by just weaving the closures through a large portion of the line rather than the entire thing. You may feel this will work better and remain tighter over the long haul.

Work on utilizing the two models and you will discover what works best for you!

CHAPTER 10

The Double Crochet Stitch

The double crochet stitch is the second most normal crochet stitch. It comprises of two single knit lines in tallness, however it isn't exactly as close as the single crochet stitch. The double crochet stitch is a wonderful stitch that glances incredible in covers, caps, scarves, and sweaters.

The twofold (double) crochet is abridged (DC). This is imperative to know for design perusing.

Look down considerably further to discover itemized composed guidelines on the best way to twofold crochet.

Establishment Chain: To get familiar with this stitch, start by fastening 20 (CH 20).

Stage 1: Yarn over the snare (YO).

Stage 2: Insert your hook into the fourth chain from your hook.

Tip: When you start a stitch venture utilizing an establishment chain, you will consistently need to put your first twofold stitch into the fourth chain from your hook.

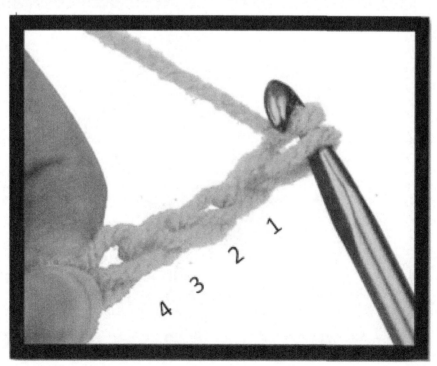

Tip: Always enter your hook into the top circle of the chain except if the example you are following requires something else.

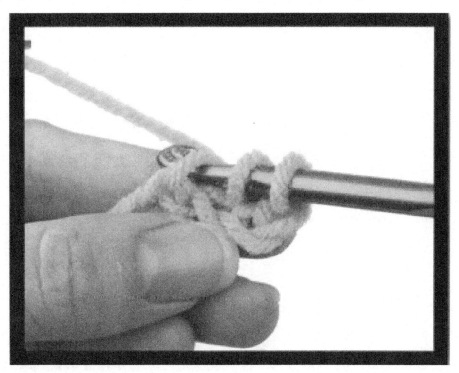

Stage 3: Yarn over the snare (YO).

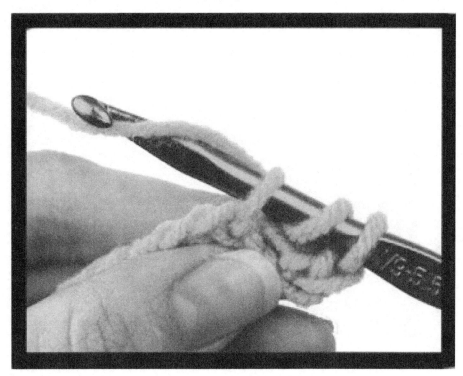

Stage 4: Pull or draw the yarn through the chain. There will presently be 3 circles on your hook.

Stage 5: Yarn over the hook (YO).

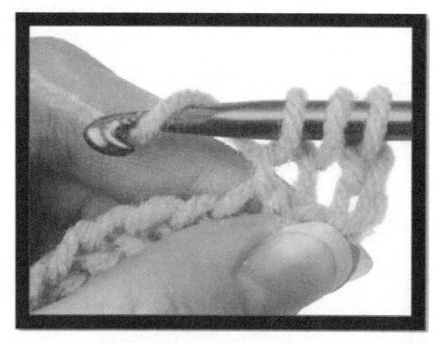

Stage 6: Pull the yarn through just the initial 2 circles on your hook and not through the last circle. The initial two circles will turn out to

be a piece of the join leaving the recently made circle on the hook and the last circle that you didn't get the yarn through. There will currently be 2 circles on your hook.

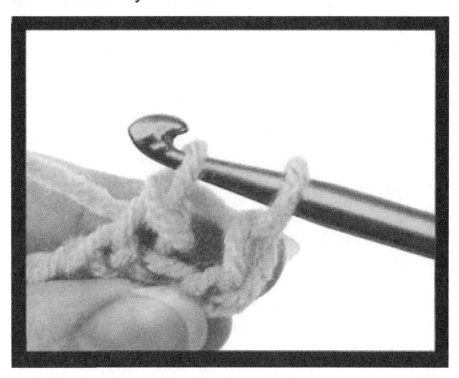

Stage 7: Yarn over the hook (YO).

Stage 8: Pull the yarn through the keep going 2 circles on your hook, and your first twofold stitch is currently finished.

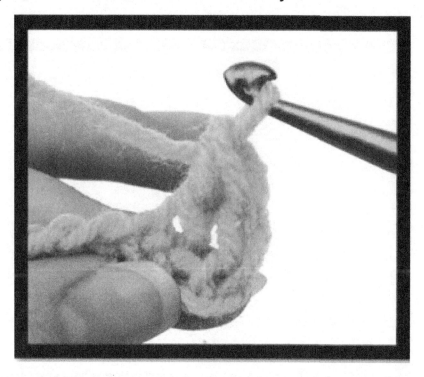

Presently wrap up the entirety of your twofold stitches into the establishment chain!!

Twofold Crochet - 2nd Row

Stage 1: Chain 3, and turn your work around (CH 3).

Tip: When twofold stitching, you will consistently need to tie 3 when climbing a column. Recollect the chain 3 considers your first twofold knit and is likewise viewed as the turning chain.

Stage 2: Yarn over the hook (YO).

Stage 3: Insert the hook into the subsequent join, not the first line.

Tip: When twofold stitching into your subsequent column, and the entirety of the lines that follow, you will consistently need to skirt the main join and spot your first twofold knit into the subsequent fasten. This is on the grounds that the turning chain considers your first twofold crotchet.

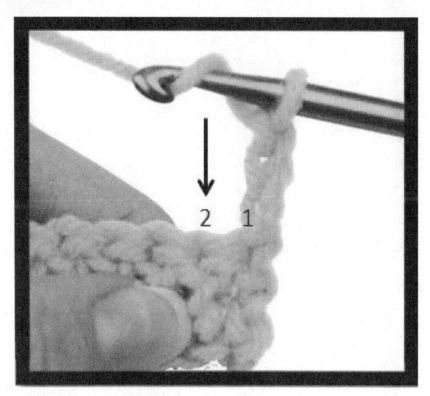

Tip: The line that you will be working in is comprised of two strands of yarn. The join resembles the letter 'V'... Line = V.

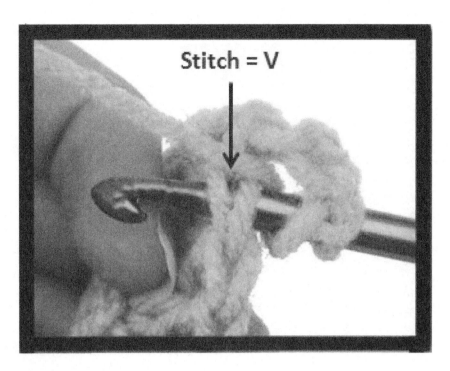

Stage 4: Yarn over the hook (YO).

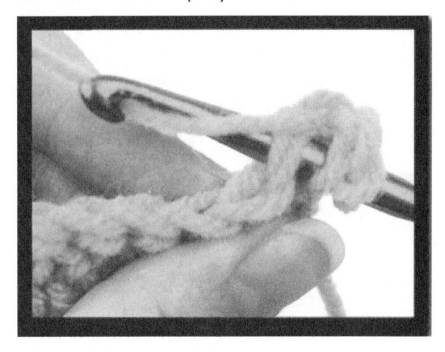

Stage 5: Pull or draw the yarn through the line. There will currently be 3 circles on your hook.

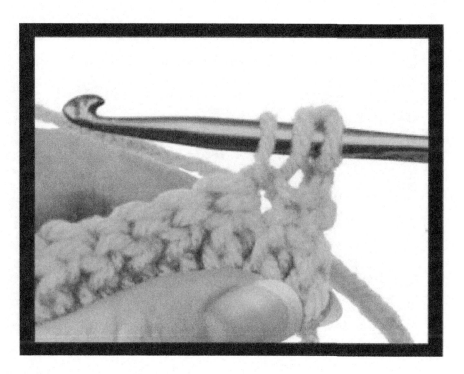

Rehash stages 5 through 8 from the primary (first) line.

The main distinction is that you will knit into the twofold crochet stitch as opposed to the establishment chain.

Last Tip: When completing your columns, make sure to work your last twofold crochet stitch into the turning chain.

CHAPTER 11

Figure out How to Half Double Crochet

T he half double crochet is a stitch that is fun and simple to learn, and it glances incredible in caps and headbands in light of its cozy stitching. The contraction for this stitch is (HDC).

Follow the exercise beneath to gain proficiency with the initial two columns of this line. After you become familiar with the initial two lines you ought to have the option to achieve anyway numerous columns you like with no issues.

Half Double – 1ˢᵗ Row

Establishment Chain: To get familiar with this start, start by binding 20 (CH 20).

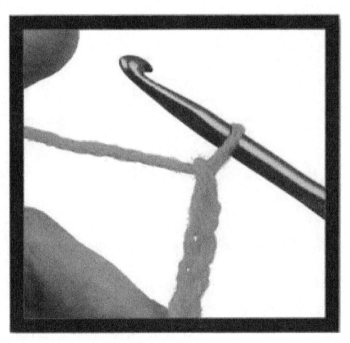

Stage 1: Yarn over the hook (YO).

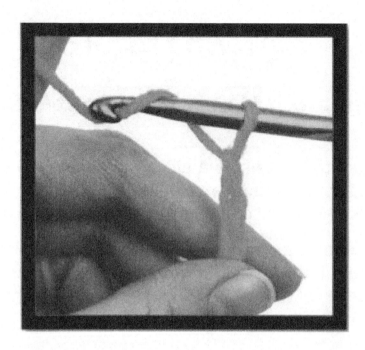

Stage 2: Place your hook into the third chain from your hook.

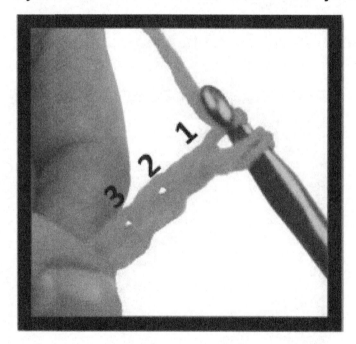

Tip: When setting the half twofold stitch into the establishment chain, you will consistently need to put this line into the third chain from your hook. You will wind up with the first 2 circles over the hook with the third circle from the chain.

Another Tip: Always enter your hook into the top circle of the chain except if the pattern you are following requires something else.

Stage 3: Yarn over the hook (YO).

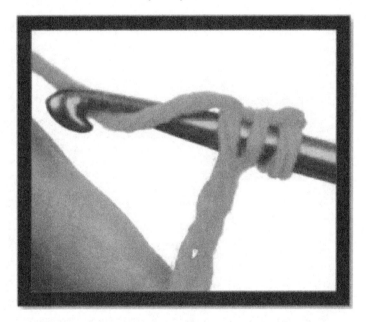

Stage 4: Draw the yarn through the chain. You will presently have 3 circles on your hook.

Stage 5: Yarn over the hook (YO).

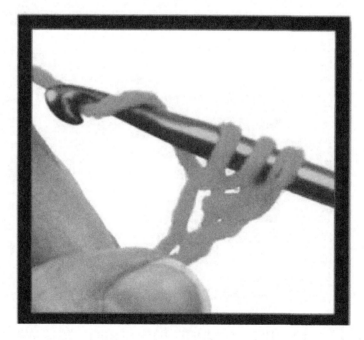

Stage 6: Draw the yarn through every one of the 3 circles on your hook.

Congrats you have recently finished your first half twofold line! Presently keep putting this line into the remainder of the establishment chain.

Half Double - 2ⁿᵈ Row

Stage 1a: Chain 2, and turn your work around (CH 2).

Tip: When utilizing this line, you will consistently need to tie 2 when climbing a line. Recollect the chain 2 considers your first join and is additionally viewed as the turning chain.

Stage 1b: Yarn over the hook (YO).

Stage 2: Place the hook into the subsequent fasten.

Tip: Always avoid the principal line and spot your first half twofold stitch into the subsequent fasten. This is on the grounds that the turning chain considers your first line.

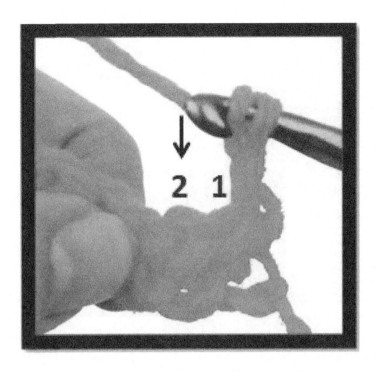

Tip: The fasten that you will be working in is comprised of two strands of yarn. The join resembles the letter 'V'... V = Stitch.

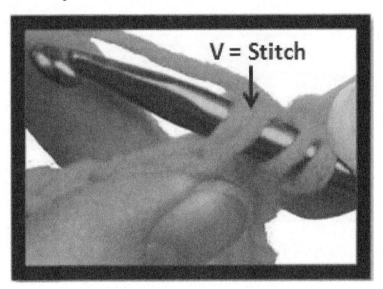

Stage 3: Yarn over the hook (YO).

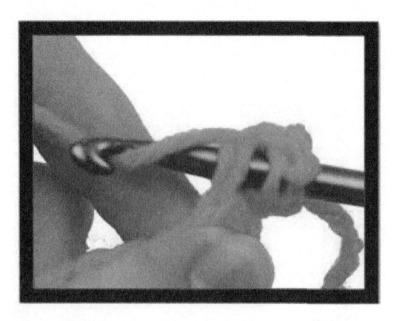

Stage 4: Pull or draw the yarn through the join. There will currently be 3 circles on your hook.

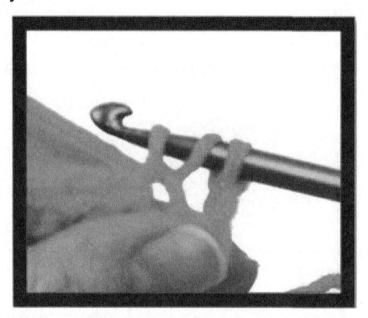

Rehash stages 5 through 6 from the primary line.

The main contrast is that you will knit into the line as opposed to the establishment chain.

Tip: When completing your lines, make sure to work your last fasten into the turning chain.

CHAPTER 12

The Treble or Triple Crochet Stitch

The triple crochet fasten (stitch) condensed (TR), is additionally called treble crotchet stitch. The term triple is generally utilized in the United States, however on the off chance that you hear the word treble crochet stitch, you will currently comprehend its significance.

The triple knit is extraordinary stitch that is generally utilized for a more loosened up stitch venture. The purpose behind this is on the grounds that it delivers a more free and transparent sort impact. I for one love utilizing the triple stitch for weaving lace all through its fastens. However, I have likewise observed it utilized for free sweaters, wraps, and scarves.

Triple/Treble Crochet – 1st Row

Establishment Chain: To become familiar with this stitch, start by chaining 15 (CH 15).

Stage 1: Yarn over the hook multiple times (YO twice).

Stage 2: Place your hook into the fifth chain from your hook.

Tip: When setting the triple/treble crochet stitch into the establishment chain, you will consistently need to put this fasten into the fifth chain from your hook.

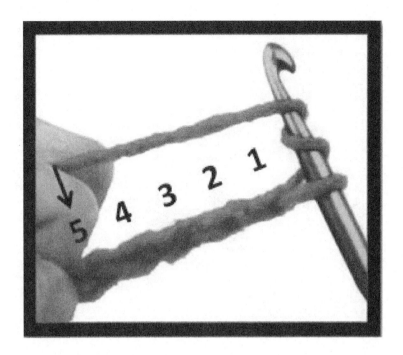

Another Tip: Always enter your hook into the top circle of the chain except if the pattern you are following requires something else.

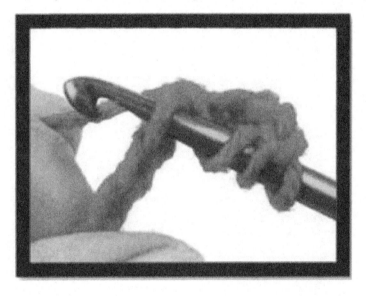

Stage 3: Yarn over the snare (YO).

Stage 4: Pull or draw the yarn just through the chain you just entered. There will presently be 4 circles on your hook.

Stage 5: Yarn over the hook (YO).

Stage 6: Only get the yarn through the initial 2 circles on your hook. There will currently be 3 circles on your hook.

Stage 7: Yarn over the hook (YO).

Stage 8: Only get the yarn through the following 2 circles on your hook.

There should now be 2 circles on your hook.

Stage 9: Yarn over the hook (YO).

Stage 10: Pull the yarn through the keep going 2 circles on your hook.

Great job! You have now finished your first triple crochet stitch! Finish setting this stitch into the establishment chain and afterward proceed onward to the subsequent line.

Triple/Treble Crochet - 2nd Row

Stage 1: Chain 4, and turn your work around (CH 4).

Tip: When triple stitching, you will consistently need to tie 4 when climbing a line. Recall the chain 4 considers your first triple crochet stitch, and is additionally called the turning chain.

Stage 2: Yarn over the hook multiple times (YO twice).

Stage 3: Place the hook into the subsequent stitch. Recall you as of now have your first stitch since you anchored 4.

Tip: The line that you will be working in is comprised of two strands of yarn. The stitch resembles the letter 'V'... V = Stitch.

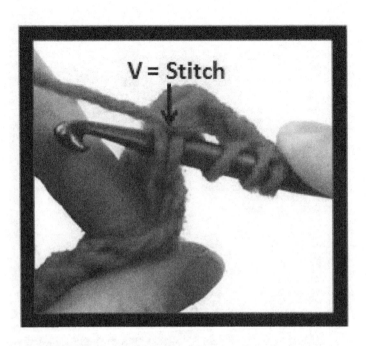

Stage 4: Yarn over the hook (YO).

Stage 5: Pull or draw the yarn through the line. There will currently be 4 circles on your hook.

Rehash steps 5 through 10 from the primary column.

Tip: Remember that on the subsequent column and the entirety of the lines that follow, you will knit into the line instead of the establishment chain.

Printed in Great Britain
by Amazon

35261186R00057